Written by

Sam Berman

Book Title

"Effortless Enterprise: Strategies for Simplifying and Succeeding in Business"

Contents

Chapter 1: The Simplicity Imperative

- A key tenet of "The Simplicity Imperative" is that simplicity is not merely a plus in the corporate world; rather, it is a precondition for achievement. This idea supports the view that, for maximum efficiency and effectiveness, businesses should give top priority to simplifying their procedures, offerings, and strategy as a whole.

-
  Business decision-making, communication, product design, customer experience, and even organizational structure may all benefit from a focus on simplicity, as suggested by the imperative. Simplifying processes, products, and services in order to better serve customers and respond to market changes is seen as a crucial business strategy.

- The Simplicity Imperative is a set of principles that helps organizations prioritize what's most important in a world where there's often too much information and too much complication. One way to achieve this goal is to reduce the complexity of related processes, products, and lines of communication. The objective is to streamline processes so they don't get in the way of work or slow down the company's capacity to adapt to shifting market conditions.

- The simplicity imperative has been shown to have good effects on both internal operations and consumer satisfaction for businesses that identify and use it. A favorable brand image and devoted client base are the results of providing clear and uncomplicated products or services, communication, and decision-making procedures.

- In sum, the Simplicity Imperative represents a strategic outlook that understands simplicity to be a key differentiator in today's economic world.

In order to succeed in today's competitive and uncertain market, firms must regularly assess and streamline their processes.

- **Chapter 2: The Blueprint of Simplicity**

- For businesses, "The Blueprint of Simplicity" is a blueprint or structure that specifies how simplicity should be implemented across the board. It's a manual for businesses that want to streamline their processes, offerings, and strategies. This strategy document is meant to serve as a road map for businesses as they try to make sense of and succeed in today's increasingly complex business climate.

-

The Blueprint of Simplicity is the idea of developing a methodical and deliberate plan for streamlining crucial corporate functions like decision-making, communication, and process flow. Some of the more prominent parts of the blueprint for simplicity are as follows:

- Purpose Statement: Clearly articulate the organization's raison d'etre. Find out what your company stands for and what it hopes to accomplish.

- Process streamlining identifies and removes any extraneous or complex procedures from existing business processes. Streamlining processes can improve efficiency and cut down on expenses.

- Products and services that are user-friendly are created with the consumer in mind. Focus on making the product's features, interfaces, and overall use as easy as possible for the user.

- Establish channels of communication that are open and honest. Make sure that everyone who needs to understand your internal and external communications can.

- Simplifying decision-making processes can help foster a culture of agility in decision-making. Empower teams to make educated decisions quickly without excessive bureaucracy.

- An organizational structure that can easily adjust to new circumstances needs to be created. Reduce organizational structure and foster teamwork between divisions.

- Adopt a philosophy of constant development and growth. Examine methods, items, and approaches frequently to spot places where they might be simplified or improved.

- Use technology to your advantage by streamlining and automating mundane processes. Improve productivity and efficiency by using the appropriate tools and processes.

- The Blueprint for Simplicity may help any firm become more nimble, responsive, and customer-focused. The objective is to lay the groundwork for continued success despite increasing competition, shifting consumer preferences, and other external factors. To help businesses of all sizes streamline and improve their operations, the blueprint provides a flexible strategic framework that can be tailored to meet their unique requirements.

- ## Chapter 3: Streamlining Processes for Success

- The term "streamlining processes for success" is used to describe a company's deliberate attempt to improve its performance by streamlining and standardizing its many internal workflows and procedures. By streamlining their processes, firms may become more nimble, responsive, and competitive, and this idea acknowledges that the way tasks and activities are carried out substantially impacts overall business success.

- The following are some essential components of the overarching concept of "Streamlining Processes for Success":

- Gains in Efficiency: Increasing productivity is the overarching objective of every process simplification effort. In order to get things done faster and cheaper, it's important to root out and get rid of any workflow inefficiencies you may find.

- Streamlining procedures usually results in more efficient use of available resources. Organizations can make better use of their time, personnel, and other resources if they streamline their processes and maximize their usage of available resources.

- Saving money: streamlining operations can have this effect. In order to run a business more efficiently and save money, it may be essential to eliminate some costs, reduce others, and reallocate others.

- Decisions can be made more quickly. Complex processes often slow people down. By minimizing the amount of time spent on information gathering and analysis, streamlining procedures allows for more rapid decision-making.

- The quality of a product or service can be enhanced by streamlining its production. Businesses may improve their products' quality and consistency by lowering the risk of mistakes and slowdowns.

- Organizational agility is increased because of streamlined Procedures. In today's fast-paced business world, where meeting the changing needs of both the market and your customers requires lightning-fast reactions, this is more important than ever.

- The satisfaction of your consumers might be increased by streamlining your procedures. An improved customer experience is the result of optimized operations across the board, from order processing to customer service.

- Simplifying procedures is one way to foster an environment that encourages creative thinking. Teams are better able to think outside the box and come up with novel solutions when they are not bogged down by unneeded complexity.

- Organizations often undertake process audits, collect feedback from employees, use technology to automate tasks, and continuously analyze and adjust workflows in order to streamline processes for success. The goal is to build an operating structure that is both streamlined and flexible enough to help the company thrive in the face of increasing competition.

- ## Chapter 4: Communication Clarity

- "Communication Clarity" refers to the quality of communication that is clear, easily understood, and devoid of ambiguity. It stresses the significance of communicating in a way that leaves little room for misunderstanding. Clear communication is essential in many settings, such as work, school, personal relationships, and others.

- "Communication Clarity" is characterized by the following essential features:

- Directness: Getting your point across clearly often requires cutting to the chase. To avoid confusion, it's best to cut to the chase and leave out the fluff.

- Accuracy and precision are essential for communicating ideas and concepts. The effectiveness of a communication rests in its ability to convey its intended meaning to the target audience.

- In order to reach the widest possible audience, it is important to keep the message simple and clear, which means minimizing the use of technical or industry-specific jargon. Without proper context, jargon can lead to misunderstandings.

- Choose your words with care and tailor your language to your audience to ensure that your message is received clearly. It is also crucial to take cultural and contextual considerations into account.

- The same attention to clarity should be paid to both written and verbal forms of communication. This means utilizing appropriate syntax and punctuation, a well-organized structure, and clear formatting when writing. Speaking clearly and pronouncing words correctly aid in getting your point across.

- Inviting comments and checking in with the receiver to make sure they get the point are two essential parts of making sure your message is understood. Any misunderstandings can be discussed and cleared out with such open dialogue.

- The use of visual aids, such as charts, graphs, or diagrams, can be helpful in cases where such a depiction would improve comprehension. The presence of visuals can greatly improve the understanding of what is being said or written.

- The key to effective communication is adjusting your delivery based on who you're talking to and what they already know. To make their message stick, good communicators always take into account the specifics of their target audience.

- Misunderstandings are a major source of inefficiency, uncertainty, and mistakes in the workplace, making clear communication even more crucial. Leadership, working with teams, interacting with customers, and all other forms of group and individual interaction benefit from this talent. An environment where people are able to understand one another and work together effectively is fostered when people make an effort to communicate clearly.

Chapter 5: Technological Simplicity

- The term "technological simplicity" is used to describe the practice of putting the needs of the user first in the creation, deployment, and utilization of technological systems. It personifies the concept that technological tools should be natural to use and simple in their construction. The end result should be an easier-to-use and more enjoyable technological experience for everyone.

- Examples of essential features of "technological simplicity" are:

- When creating a UI, it's important to keep things as straightforward as possible. This requires building layouts, navigation, and interactions that are intuitive and easy for people to comprehend, even without considerable training.

- Simplicity in technology focuses on making goods and systems that are intuitive to use. A better user experience is achieved by minimizing the learning curve and the amount of training required.

- Functionality, which comes naturally to consumers, is a hallmark of the most successful technologies. Intuitive design assures that people will be able to pick up and use the technology without a lot of training.

- Simplified Functions Rather than bombarding users with a laundry list of options, simplified technologies give priority to those that are most likely to be used and appreciated. This helps avoid unnecessary features and puts the emphasis where it belongs: on the needs of the user.

- Providing concise documentation Concise documentation is crucial for technological ease of use. Users should be able to quickly and easily have access to relevant documentation, FAQs, and tutorials that will help them make the most of the technology.

- Compatibility across platforms and devices is an important part of making technology easy to use. This ensures that the technology can be accessed and interacted with across a wide range of devices.

- Minimalistic Design: Adopting a minimalistic design concept, both in terms of hardware and software, adds to technological simplicity. Reducing superfluous parts, visual noise, and design complexity is part of this process.

- Flexibility: User-friendly technologies benefit from flexibility and responsiveness. Adjustable features allow users to tailor the experience to their specific needs.

- Simplifying technology is increasingly important in today's age of rapid digital innovation, when consumers are constantly exposed to new tools. To reach the widest possible audience, developers and designers must strike a balance between the complexity of their solutions and the ease with which they may be implemented. This method has the potential to boost the efficiency, satisfaction, and uptake of technology solutions.

Chapter 6: Customer-Centric Simplicity

- The term "customer-centric simplicity" is used to describe a method of doing business that prioritizes the ease and satisfaction of the customer experience. The idea behind this term is that customers are more likely to be satisfied with a company and remain loyal if they have a positive experience doing business with that organization. Keeping things easy for the consumer means creating processes, goods, and services from their point of view and requirements.

- Features integral to customer-centric simplicity are:

- Creating products and services with the end user in mind means prioritizing issues like usability and accessibility. This includes reducing complexity as much as possible, providing easy-to-use interfaces, and making sure customers can get what they need from the products or services.

- Communicating with clients in a way that is unambiguous, open, and simple to grasp. When it comes to marketing, product descriptions, and contacts with customer service, clarity is key to building trust and happy customers.

- Customization, or personalization, is the process of making goods and services fit the specific wants and needs of each buyer. Businesses may make customers' decision-making processes easier by anticipating and meeting their needs in the form of more customized and relevant experiences.

- Quick and effective problem-solving is the result of streamlining the customer care process. This includes providing accessible help channels, clear instructions, and responsive assistance.

- Streamlining the buying procedure will reduce friction and increase efficiency. This includes reducing the number of clicks required to complete a purchase, making product and pricing details easily accessible, and providing safe and flexible payment methods.

- Seeking and considering consumer input in order to better comprehend those customers' views and experiences Using this information, businesses may better understand their customers' wants and needs and adapt their products and services accordingly.

- Creating products and services that can be modified to meet the needs of a wide range of consumers is an example of adaptability. Options, service levels, or features that may be modified to fit the needs of a wide range of customers are examples of this.

- Empowering customers means giving them access to the resources they need to make wise purchases. Customers feel more valued and trusted when they are given opportunities to learn and exercise agency.

- In today's highly competitive market, customers place a premium on ease of use, transparency, and a streamlined process, and companies that embrace a customer-centric, simple strategy recognize this. Businesses can increase customer happiness, customer loyalty, and competitive advantage by tailoring their operations and products to meet the needs of their target demographic. The end goal is to make customers' interactions with your firm so satisfying that they want to tell others about it.

Chapter 7: Agile Decision-Making

- In the face of uncertainty and change, "agile decision-making" is a strategy wherein decisions are made swiftly, adaptively, and cooperatively inside an organization. This idea is related to the ideas of the agile technique, which was first used in software development but has now been adopted for use in other areas of business. Agile decision-making is characterized by its focus on effectively delivering value and its emphasis on flexibility and adaptability.

- Some of the most distinguishing features of agile decision-making are:

- Agile decision-making is typically an iterative, incremental procedure. Instead of making decisions in a linear manner, businesses may take tiny, iterative steps, allowing for ongoing input and modifications.

- Decision-making is a group endeavor that requires members of different departments to work together. When people with different backgrounds and experiences get together to solve a problem, they increase the likelihood that the solution will take into account all relevant factors.

- Quick Adjustment to New Circumstances: Agile decision-making functions best in fast-paced, unpredictable settings Agile approaches are used by businesses to be nimble and adaptable in the face of change and uncertainty.

- Decisions Based on Evidence and Data: The Agile Method places a premium on using available information when making choices. Decisions are more objective and less based on pure intuition when organizations collect and evaluate relevant data to inform them.

- Agile decision-making frequently puts the consumer first. Each choice is made with the end user in mind, and suggestions from those users are actively sought out and implemented whenever possible.

- Plans are seen as flexible guides as opposed to rigid constructions in an adaptive planning environment. The ability to quickly adjust strategies and priorities in light of new knowledge is a hallmark of agile companies.

- To make quick, effective decisions, open and honest dialogue is essential. Team members discuss the decision, its justification, and any potential consequences openly and honestly with one another.

- Team Autonomy: In agile decision-making, teams are given the authority to make their own choices within the boundaries of their assigned tasks. This not only facilitates quicker decision-making but also increases personal investment and accountability.

- While agile decision-making is most often linked to Scrum and Kanban, two popular agile project management frameworks, its ideas are just as applicable to organizational strategy, product development, and other business operations. Businesses may better deal with the volatility of the market, seize new opportunities as they arise, and refine their operations through the use of agile decision-making.

Chapter 8: Empowering Teams for Success

- "Empowering Teams for Success" is a leadership and management philosophy that emphasizes giving teams the freedom, authority, and resources they need to succeed. The idea recognizes that teams are more likely to be motivated, innovative, and successful when they are given autonomy; thus, it places an emphasis on trust, teamwork, and a shared sense of responsibility.

- Some of the most important factors in creating successful teams are:

- Teams with autonomy are trusted to make decisions and own their output without external oversight. Leaders encourage their teams to make well-informed decisions and offer input.

- Teams succeed when everyone knows their role and what they're trying to accomplish. When the objectives are well-defined and correspond with the broader mission of the firm, teams may focus their efforts more efficiently.

- Providing opportunities for team members to gain new skills and advance in their current roles is an important part of empowering teams. That could mean providing team members with access to training courses, workshops, and other tools that help them develop their skills.

- It is essential to set up lines of communication that are both open and transparent. Everyone on the team should feel safe voicing their opinions and providing constructive criticism. As a result, leaders need to be attentive to their teams' concerns and requirements.

- Allocation of Resources: Effective teams have all the tools they need to complete their projects. Support from other groups or stakeholders is also considered part of the necessary resources.

- It is crucial to recognize and reward team members for their efforts and accomplishments. A healthy and motivated team culture can be fostered through many forms of recognition, such as praise, promotions, or other concrete benefits.

- A culture of sharing and invention flourishes in settings where collaboration is encouraged both inside and between teams. Often, empowered teams cooperate well, drawing on each member's unique set of abilities and views to find novel solutions to difficult issues.

- The most effective teams have established methods to receive regular feedback on their performance and growth opportunities. Getting and using constructive criticism is crucial to development and progress.

- responsibility that comes with more autonomy. Everyone on the team shares equal responsibility for the results of their efforts. Teams are more likely to stay focused on their goals when they have clear expectations and accountability mechanisms in place.

- In many cases, empowered teams are better able to adjust to new circumstances. Leaders inspire followers to view setbacks not as fatalities but as learning experiences that can only strengthen their resolve to succeed in the future.

- Team empowerment is more than just delegating work; it's about making everyone feel like they belong, are trusted, and are encouraged to give their all. Evidence suggests that adopting this strategy might boost productivity, morale, and creativity within an organization.

- ## Chapter 9: Sustainable Simplicity

- The term "sustainable simplicity" is used to describe the process of adopting simple and streamlined practices that are long-term sustainable from an ecological, social, and economic perspective. It covers the belief that simplicity, when applied to various aspects of life and business, can contribute to sustainability by lowering resource consumption, minimizing waste, and fostering a balanced and resilient approach to development.

- The term "sustainable simplicity" refers to several interrelated concepts.

- Taking into account the effects on the environment is essential to achieving sustainable simplicity. This necessitates making changes that lessen our impact on the environment, such as using fewer natural resources and producing less waste. In many cases, businesses can lessen their impact on the environment and aid in conservation efforts by streamlining their processes.

- Efficiency in using resources can be achieved by streamlining both production processes and final goods. To get the same or better results while reducing the use of resources, including materials, energy, and water, it may be necessary. Natural resources can be preserved through the practice of sustainable simplicity.

- Sustainable simplicity is in line with the ideas of a circular economy, which emphasize the reuse, recycling, and repurposing of resources. As a result, we may rely less on the unsustainable and wasteful "take-make-dispose" model and more on one that is sustainable and productive.

- Equity in society is taken into account by those who practice sustainable simplicity. It entails respect for employees' rights, concern for the community, and a determination to improve everyone's standard of living. Efforts to streamline processes shouldn't compromise on efforts to increase fairness.

- Sustainable practices include giving preference to materials and goods that are locally produced or obtained in an ethical manner. Organizations can reduce their environmental impact and boost local economies by streamlining their supply chains and shortening the distance between production and consumption.

- Sustainability Sustainable simplicity looks to the future and not just the present for its value. It takes into account the resilience of systems and practices to guarantee that they can last and adapt to changing situations without jeopardizing future generations' well-being.

- Sustainability is aided by adopting minimalist ideas, which place value on owning as little as possible. This concept can be used to cut down on extras and waste in both private and commercial settings.

- Adopting and spreading the use of renewable energy is consistent with the principles of sustainable simplicity. Simplifying energy infrastructure means relying less on traditional sources and more on cleaner, more long-term options.

- Raising awareness and educating stakeholders about the benefits of simplicity and sustainability is a common component of sustainable Simplicity. Sustainable practices spread when people and businesses make well-informed decisions.

- Businesses and individuals can build practices that both simplify operations and contribute to the well-being of the planet and its inhabitants by incorporating sustainable concepts into the concept of simplicity. Sustainable simplicity reflects a holistic and responsible approach to decision-making and resource use, striving for a balance between meeting current demands and protecting the ability of future generations to meet their own needs.

Chapter 10: Future-Proofing the Effortless Enterprise

- "Future-Proofing the Effortless Enterprise" refers to the strategic efforts and considerations taken by businesses to guarantee that their operations, systems, and strategies remain relevant, adaptive, and robust in the face of future uncertainties and changes. The term "future-proofing" refers to the practice of anticipating and planning for future events in order to ensure continued success and relevance.

- Foreseeing Potential Shifts in the Business Environment, Industry Trends, and Technology Landscapes: Future-Proofing Requires an Aggressive Forward-Looking Approach Companies can better position themselves for the future if they are aware of and prepared for rising trends.

- Future-proofing requires an organization to adopt new technology and find ways to use them. Methods such as automation, artificial intelligence, and cutting-edge hardware and software may be implemented to increase productivity while decreasing overhead and making businesses more competitive.

- Future-proof businesses frequently embrace agile and adaptive methods that allow them to adjust quickly to shifts in the market. This entails being flexible enough to adapt to changing circumstances, try out novel approaches, and fine-tune tactics in response to immediate input.

- Growth of Talent: Preparing for the Future Requires the Creation of a Skilled and Flexible Workforce In order to keep up with the rapid changes in technology and market demands, businesses must provide their staff with the knowledge and abilities necessary to do their jobs effectively.

- Future-proofing hinges on anticipating and meeting the changing demands of your customers. Businesses may better meet the ever-evolving demands of their customers if they take a customer-first approach to all they do.

- To prepare for the future, sustainability initiatives must take environmental and social factors into account. Adapting to new regulations and shifting consumer tastes is easier for businesses that have adopted sustainable practices.

- Future-proofing requires strong cybersecurity measures to protect against future threats, especially given our growing reliance on digital technologies. Keeping people's faith in systems and information requires diligent, preventative security measures.

- Businesses that are prepared for the future incorporate operational flexibility into their daily routines. Possible solutions include making infrastructure and supply chains more flexible and responsive to changes in demand and market conditions.

- Strategic Partnerships: Collaborating with strategic partners can strengthen future-proofing initiatives. In today's dynamic business environment, partnerships are essential for firms to leverage complementary knowledge, exchange resources, and collectively address difficulties.

- Future-proofing requires a commitment to a culture of constant innovation. As part of this effort, we must inspire our staff to think outside the box, try something different, and help foster an environment where innovation and flexibility thrive.

- By integrating these strategies, businesses may build what they call an "efficient enterprise" that streamlines current processes while also ensuring their continued viability, flexibility, and competitiveness in the long run. Strategies that future-proof businesses use prepare them for change and help them prosper in the face of uncertainty.

www.ingramcontent.com/pod-product-compliance
Lightning Source LLC
Chambersburg PA
CBHW071008260726
48661CB00007B/2852